How to Raise

by EVELYN MILLER

Contents

1. POODLE STANDARDS 3
Varieties of poodles . . . American poodle standards . . . English poodle standards

2. BRINGING YOUR PUPPY HOME 10
Harness and lead . . . Food for your puppy . . . A place for your puppy to sleep . . . Vitamins and minerals

3. GROOMING YOUR POODLE 14
Tools necessary . . . Bathing . . . The Puppy Clip . . . English Saddle Clip . . . Continental Clip . . . Royal Dutch Clip . . . Kennel Clip . . . Do's and don't's of clipping your poodle

4. HOW TO TRAIN YOUR DOG 31
Animal or pet? . . . Dog owner's part . . . Giving commands . . . What about lessons? . . . What you will teach your dog . . . How to housebreak your puppy . . . Collar and leash . . . Training your dog to walk properly . . . to come to you . . . to stay at your side . . . to stop without command . . . Off-the-leash training . . . Teaching your dog to sit . . . to lie down . . . to stay . . . Discipline training . . . Keeping your dog off the furniture . . . Training not to bark . . . to do tricks . . . to retrieve . . . not to jump on people

5. HOW TO KEEP YOUR POODLE HEALTHY 57
Eating foreign particles . . . Loss of appetite . . . Tooth disorders . . . Ear disorders . . . Various diseases . . . How to weigh your dog . . . Your veterinarian

ISBN 0-87666-355-2

Distributed in the U.S.A. by T.F.H. Publications, Inc., 211 West Sylvania Avenue, P.O. Box 27, Neptune City, N.J. 07753; in England by T.F.H. (Gt. Britain) Ltd., 13 Nutley Lane, Reigate, Surrey; in Canada to the book store and library trade by Clarke, Irwin & Company, Clarwin House, 791 St. Clair Avenue West, Toronto 10, Ontario; in Canada to the pet trade by Rolf C. Hagen Ltd., 3225 Sartelon Street, Montreal 382, Quebec; in Southeast Asia by Y.W. Ong, 9 Lorong 36 Geylang, Singapore 14; in Australia and the south Pacific by Pet Imports Pty. Ltd., P.O. Box 149, Brookvale 2100, N.S.W., Australia. Published by T.F.H. Publications, Inc. Ltd., The British Crown Colony of Hong Kong.

1. Poodle Standards

The poodle is one of the best-known breeds in the history of dogdom. It is believed to have originated in Russia where black standard-sized poodles were used as water retrievers for bird hunters. The Russians called the dog "pudel" which literally means "splashing in water." The breed spread to Northern Germany where the brown color was introduced. German artists as early as the 15th century illustrated the poodle, and the great Spanish artist, Goya, used this breed in several of his paintings. The first evidence of a toy poodle's existence came from England, where the "White Cuban" breed, said to have originated in Cuba, became an English favorite. Queen Anne had several poodles during her reign in the early 18th century.

How then did we get the name "French Poodle"? Just when the breed was introduced into France, and by whom, is still a mystery, but the French found that by clipping the hair off the body, and leaving it on the paws, the dog managed himself better in the water. A good deal of speculation about how the dog should be clipped led to the present types of clips.

We know that the poodle is not a new breed and it has definitely not been bred down in size. The toy poodle existed at about the same time as the larger sizes.

VARIETIES OF POODLES

Poodles come in three sizes under American standards: Toy, Miniature and Standard.

The Toy poodle is 10 inches or under (American rules) at the shoulder; the Miniature poodle must be under 15 inches (and more than 10 inches); and the Standard poodle must be 15 inches or over. It has been the trend to breed small Toys, large Standards and medium-sized Miniatures.

Color varieties are many. Blacks, whites, silvers, blues, chocolates and apricots are some of the desirable colors. Parti-colors are undesirable in the poodle and such dogs are disqualified from the show ring. The chocolates and apricots may have brown points, though most people prefer them to have black points, and the toenails should either be black or the color of the coat.

The most popular poodle is the pet-quality, miniature such as Samson, the silver miniature belonging to the author.

The following standards, adopted by the Poodle Club of America and approved by the American Kennel Club on May 12, 1953 are interesting to appraise your own poodle or to keep in mind when purchasing a puppy.

AMERICAN POODLE STANDARDS

GENERAL APPEARANCE, CARRIAGE AND CONDITION: That of a very active, intelligent, smart and elegant-looking dog, squarely built, well-proportioned and carrying himself proudly. Properly clipped in the traditional fashion and carefully groomed, the poodle has about him an air of distinction and dignity peculiar to himself.

HEAD AND EXPRESSION: (a) *Skull*—Should be slightly full and moderately peaked with a slight stop. Cheekbones and muscles flat. Eyes set far enough apart to indicate ample brain capacity. (b) *Muzzle*—Long, straight and fine, but strong without lippiness. The chin definite enough to preclude

Poodles are recognized in almost every solid color as far as the kennel clubs are concerned, but poodles having two or more colors on their bodies are not recognized and therefore cannot be entered in any kennel club competition. The poodles shown here are parti-colors and even though they cannot be shown in a dog show, they may be sold for more money than acceptable colored dogs!

snipiness. Teeth white, strong and level. Nose sharp with well-defined nostrils. (c) *Eyes*—Oval shape, very dark, full of fire and intelligence. (d) *Ears*—Set low and hanging close to the head. The leather long, wide and heavily feathered—when drawn forward almost reaches the nose.

NECK—Well-proportioned, strong and long enough to admit of the head being carried high and with dignity. Skin snug at throat.

SHOULDERS—Strong, muscular, angulated at the point of the shoulder and the elbow joint sloping well back.

BODY—The chest deep and moderately wide. The ribs well sprung and braced up. The back short, strong and very slightly hollowed, with the loins broad and muscular. (Bitches may be slightly longer in back than dogs.)

TAIL—Set on rather high, docked and carried gaily. Never curled or carried over the back.

LEGS—The forelegs straight from shoulders with plenty of bone and muscle. Hind legs very muscular, stifles well bent, and hocks well let down. Hindquarters well developed with the second thigh showing both width and muscle.

FEET—Rather small and of good oval shape. Toes well arched and close, pad thick and hard.

COAT—(a) *Quality*—Curly poodles: very profuse, of harsh texture, even length, frizzy or curly, not at all open. Corded poodles: very thick, hanging in tight, even cords. (b) *Clip*—Clipping either in the traditional "Continental" or "English Saddle" style is correct. In the Continental clip the hindquarters are shaved, with pompoms on hips (optional), and in the English Saddle clip, the hindquarters are covered with a short blanket of hair. In both these clips the rest of the body must be left in full coat. The face, feet, legs and tail must be shaved, leaving bracelets on all four legs, and a pompom at the end of the tail. The topknot and feather on the ears must be long and profuse, so as not to lose the very essential poodle expression. A dog under a year old may be shown with the coat long except the face, feet and base of tail, which should be shaved. Any poodle clipped in any style other than the above-mentioned shall be disqualified from the show ring.

COLOR—Any solid color. All but the browns have black noses, lips and eyelids. The browns and apricots may have liver noses and dark amber eyes. In all colors, toenails either black or the same color as the dog.

Gray Poodles, whose coats have not cleared to an even, solid color, may be shown up to the age of 18 months. The degree of clearing shall only count in judging two or more gray Poodles under the age of 18 months when all other points are equal, in which case the more completely cleared dog shall be judged superior.

GAIT—A straightforward trot with light springy action. Head and tail carried high.

VALUE OF POINTS:

General appearance, carriage and condition	20
Head, ears, eyes and expression	20

Neck and shoulders	10
Body and tail	15
Legs and feet	10
Coat, color and texture	15
Gait	10

So long as the dog is definitely a Miniature or a Toy, diminutiveness is only the deciding factor when all other points are equal; soundness and activity are every bit as necessary in a Miniature and a Toy as they are in a Standard poodle, and as these traits can only be seen when the dog is in action, it is imperative that Miniatures and Toys be moved in the ring as fully and decidedly as Standard poodles.

MAJOR FAULTS—Bad mouth—either undershot or overshot; cow-hocks; flat or spread feet, thin pads, very light eyes; excessive shyness; monorchidism.

DISQUALIFICATIONS—Parti-colors; unorthodox-clip; cryptorchidism.

ENGLISH POODLE STANDARDS

GENERAL APPEARANCE—That of a very active, intelligent, and elegant-looking dog, well-built, carrying himself very proudly.

HEAD AND SKULL—Head long and straight and fine, the skull not broad, with a slight peak at the back. Muzzle long (but not snipy) and strong —not full in cheek, lips black and not showing lippiness. Nose back and sharp.

EYES—Almond-shape, very dark, full of fire and intelligence.

EARS—The leather long and wide, low set on, hanging close to the face.

MOUTH—Teeth white, strong and level.

NECK—Well-proportioned and strong, to admit of the head being carried high and with dignity.

FOREQUARTERS—Shoulders strong and muscular, sloping well to the back. Legs straight from the shoulder with plenty of bone and muscle.

BODY—Chest deep and moderately wide. Back short, strong and slightly hollowed, the loins broad and muscular, the ribs well sprung and braced up.

HINDQUARTERS—Legs very muscular and bent, with the hocks well let down.

FEET—Rather small and of good shape, the toes well arched, pads thick and hard.

TAIL—Set on rather high, well carried, never curled or carried over the back.

COAT—Very profuse and of good, hard texture; if corded, hanging in tight, even cords; if non-corded, very thick and strong of even length, the curls close and thick without knots or cords. It is strongly recommended that the traditional English Saddle clip should be adhered to.

COLOR—All black, all white, all brown, all blue. The white poodle should have dark eyes, black nose, lips and toenails. The brown poodle should have dark amber eyes, dark liver nose, lips and toenails. The blue poodle should be of even color, and have dark eyes, lips and toenails. All the other points of white, brown and blue poodles should be the same as the perfect black poodle.

WEIGHT AND SIZE—Standard poodles: 15 inches and over; Miniature poodles: under 15 inches.

FAULTS—In the Miniature poodle: heavy build, clumsiness, long back, light, round and prominent eyes, bad stern carriage, heavy gait, coarse head, over- or undershot mouth, flesh-colored nose, coarse legs and feet, open and rusty coats, white markings on black and colored poodles, lemon or other markings on white poodles.

The standards issued by the American and English Kennel Clubs are concerned, unfortunately, only with physical characteristics. A dog's intelligence or personality are not judged or standardized. A pet dog must be intelligent and trainable.

Miniature poodles are so popular because they are great housepets in terms of size and strength. Samson, the author's silver poodle, is a miniature and has been taught to catch and balance his "squeak" toy.

2. Bringing Your Puppy Home

When you bring your puppy home, you will need certain items to maintain him properly.

1. A harness (or collar) and lead (or leash)
2. Food
3. A suitable dog bed
4. A suitable set of feeding dishes
5. Toys to teethe on and play with
6. Comb and brush
7. Suitable bathing accessories
8. Vitamin and mineral supplement

THE HARNESS AND LEAD

Harnesses are usually made of leather. The cost of the harness depends upon whether the leather is double thickness or single, and whether it is studded or not. A double leather studded harness is much more costly than a single leather, plain. For the growing puppy you can use either type to good advantage. Young puppies love to chew and if they can find nothing better, they will chew on the harness. If the harness is strong and studded, a puppy will be discouraged from chewing because of the metal and the stiffness of the leather. A good hour-long chew will ruin a single leather harness.

On the other hand, a young puppy grows rather fast and in a month or two he might easily outgrow a good harness, so maybe a cheaper harness would be more practical. The decision is up to you.

A harness is placed over the shoulders of a puppy. It is supposedly more humane than a collar, which goes around a puppy's neck. It is the experience of many dog lovers that a puppy is more easily trained with a collar than a harness, but you can judge that for yourself. (See chapter on training.)

A lead or leash is the piece of chain or leather that connects the puppy to you. It should be 4 to 6 feet long and durable. A light chain is very satisfactory and, depending upon the quality of the chain, can either be cheap or expensive. Since the lead can be used as long as it lasts, it is definitely advisable to spend a few extra dollars and get a fine lead, one that will not break, and will be comfortable for both yourself and the dog.

FOOD FOR YOUR PUPPY

When you have bought your dog, the person you purchase him from should give you the diet he has been maintained on up to this time. Keep him on the same diet as long as recommended.

A puppy should be fed four times a day. In the morning give him some milk (not cold) with a little cereal or egg added (plus some vitamins and minerals). About noon feed him his heavy meal of canned dog food, table scraps, cooked horsemeat, egg biscuit or dry dog food mixed with milk, broth, or water. About five in the afternoon give him a little more milk and cereal or fine dog food or egg. Before you retire, some more milk should be offered.

Keep up this diet until the puppy is 4 or 5 months old, then gradually skip the evening milk and the morning milk. When the dog is 6 or 7 months old he can be given the heavy meal in the morning and some milk fortified with vitamins and minerals in the evening. If your puppy doesn't seem to be thriving on this diet, have your vet check him over and give you a more specific diet.

All food offered to your dog should be clean and fresh, neither too hot nor too cold. Feed your puppy at the same time each day and remove whatever food he leaves behind. Don't allow the food to remain on the floor until he finally eats it. On the floor it gets dirty, dusty and stale, and you will soon have a sick dog.

Once you have selected a brand of dog food stick to it. Sometimes a change in diet will give a dog loose bowels.

The question is often asked: "Why is one dog biscuit so cheap and the other so expensive?" The answer is simple. Some dog food companies manufacture their products as by-products from other sources. For example: some manufacturers of bread, when faced with a lot of stale bread, sell it for grinding up and making into dog biscuits. On the other hand, many dog food companies go out and buy top grade wheat. They prepare their dog biscuits according to a strict formula so that every time you buy their brand you get the same recipe. The latter type of dog food is naturally more expensive, but it is worth the difference because it will keep your dog healthier and happier.

Always look at the label and check the protein content of the dog food you buy. The higher the protein content in the biscuit the more food content the dog can utilize (the remainder is mainly water and indigestible roughage and ash). Thus if brand A sells for 25c per pound and has 25% protein, and brand B is 40c per pound and has 50% protein, you're getting a bargain by buying the 40c brand. Your poodle will have to eat twice as much of brand A to get the nutrition he needs. That's why some dogs are always eating (and having to relieve themselves). Remember: There is more waste in cheap dog food!

A PLACE FOR YOUR PUPPY TO SLEEP

Every dog likes to have a place that means *home.* To a dog there is nothing more sacred than his own little bed. Even a cardboard box, with just a few torn newspapers will serve, as long as there is sufficient room for the puppy to stretch out. If you really want to make him feel like royalty, give your puppy a bed he will appreciate, a nice dog bed, made especially for the purpose, with sweet-smelling cedar shavings in his mattress, to keep the odor and the fleas away.

Locate your dog's bed on the floor away from drafts. A dark corner is good enough. Many people like to put the bed behind a chair where no one will see and disturb your sleeping puppy. Placing the bed near food is not a good idea because then your Royal Canine Highness will get into the bad habit of dragging his food into his bed to eat it. Feed him in a different room if possible.

If your new puppy prefers to sleep with you instead of alone, you have no one but yourself to blame. The little pup's first night in his new home is likely to be a memorable one for all. After spending five weeks of life with a bunch of cuddly fellow puppies and a nice warm snuggly mother, he has been cruelly taken into a foreign environment, and now he has to sleep alone and be cold! However, you must be heartless that first night. Let him howl and cry. If you have a noisy alarm clock and an old doll, place them into his bed with him and let him sleep with some company. The alarm clock will make a comforting noise and the doll will be something to snuggle with. If you break down and take him to bed with you, he will keep you awake most of the night kissing your face and your feet and you will then have started something that will be harder to correct the longer it goes on.

Every poodle needs a collar. Special poodle collars are available at your local petshop. Buy your supplies from a man who makes his living selling pet supplies as he has the best quality products, usually, and he is there if you have a complaint.

The author training her dog not to "beg" for food at the table. Never feed your dog from the table. Human food is not good for the poodle and the dog can be a nuisance when you have company.

VITAMINS AND MINERALS

Most house pets do not get a balanced diet. Their teeth get soft, their beautiful coat gets dull and shaggy and they lack the pep and vigor that is so characteristic of the breed.

Usually this is only a run-down feeling that your pet develops because he is not getting enough sunshine, proper exercise and diet. To offset this, give your dog a diet supplemented with vitamins and minerals. Visit your pet supplier and get some of these health preparations. There is a preparation (pervinal) with all the necessary vitamins and minerals in one formula. It is to be hoped that soon a manufacturer might add some of these supplements to dog food (like vitamins are added to milk).

3. Grooming Your Poodle

A poodle is *not* a poodle without proper grooming. Although poodle grooming may be a very drastic alteration of the dog's original, natural appearance, fortunately, you can choose from a wide variety of styles, and one is bound to suit your individual taste.

There are two varieties of clip allowed for fully grown poodles in the show ring: The English Saddle and the Continental. For puppies (a poodle under a year is considered a puppy) grooming is also a necessity, as no puppy is allowed into the show ring unless he is wearing a Puppy Clip.

These are not the only clips you can utilize. The Kennel Clip, though disallowed in the ring, is an easy, comfortable trim which retains most of the poodle's characteristics. The Royal Dutch Clip, my own favorite clip for non-show dogs, does not accentuate many of the poodle's features, but it has been accepted by so many breeders and fanciers that it is quite common.

Before we go into the fine points of each of these clips, you should know that clipping and grooming a poodle is far from the easiest thing in the world. Experience is necessary not only in handling the tools of the trade, but in knowing what to clip and how to clip it.

TOOLS NECESSARY FOR GROOMING YOUR POODLE

CLIPPERS: Small animal clipper, either electric or hand operated, is a necessity. Make sure that the heads are detachable and that you hold the head flat and not tilting, when using it. When cutting in between the toes or around the eyes or lips, still hold the clipper flat, but use only the edge of the machine. Get five blades as accessories to your clipper. Here are the recommended sizes and their uses:

#5 and #7—The #5 leaves the hair from $\frac{1}{4}$ to 1 inch in thickness while the #7 trims it 50% shorter. Can be used for the Kennel and Royal Dutch Clip for winter months.

#10—A finer blade than the #5 or #7, it clips the coat to $\frac{1}{8}$-$\frac{1}{16}$ of an inch in height. It leaves just enough hair on the poodle so that his skin does not show through. It can be used for the Royal Dutch and Kennel clips for the summer months. Use this blade, if you can, when giving your poodle his first trim as it is very comfortable for you and your pet.

#15—The best all-round blade for clipping your poodle. Many people have only this #15 blade and it serves their purposes well. It can do every job that has to be done on the poodle, even his face and toes. Sometimes a #30 is used for really very fine grooming for the show ring. (A beginner should have all the blades.)

A clipper must be worked according to the blade on its head. If using the #15 or #30, cut against the "grain" (the way the hair grows). The #10 can be used either way, but the #7 and #5 should be used with the grain. Naturally when you cut with the grain the blade will move faster and not cut so closely. If you use the #15 with the grain, it will have the same effect as using the #10 against the grain.

SCISSORS: Get two pairs of barber's scissors with very sharp blades. One pair should have a blunt point, and will be used for clipping the hair around the ears and the face. Also get one with a sharp point, which will be used for getting little hairs between the toes and general trimming.

COMB: A comb is very necessary to get the knots and tangles out of the poodle's coat prior to and after clipping. A good poodle comb should have round teeth about 3 inches long. Get three combs: fine, medium and coarse.

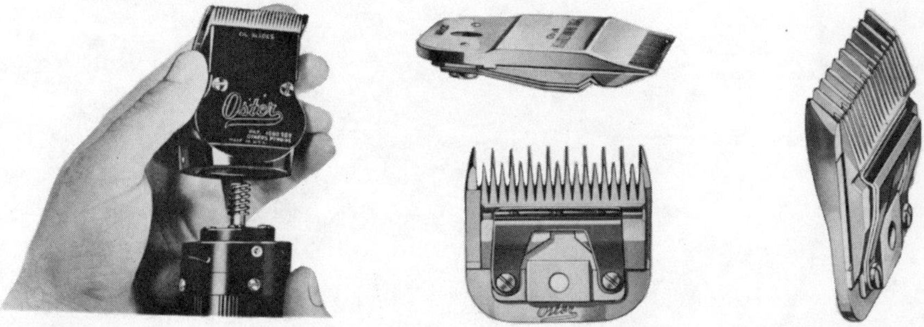

The Oster electric clipper is designed for clipping small animals (Model A-2). It has many advantages over the manual-type hand clipper and is a lot less tiring.

Grooming your own poodle is not difficult once the dog has been professionally groomed a few times. The professional groomer "breaks in" the dog to the sound of the clipper and it is easier to follow the style originally made by the professional.

The whole family should be involved in grooming the poodle . . . and the grooming should be kept up on a periodic basis. A poodle should be regularly bathed and trimmed; brushing should be done as often as possible, even every day if you have the time.

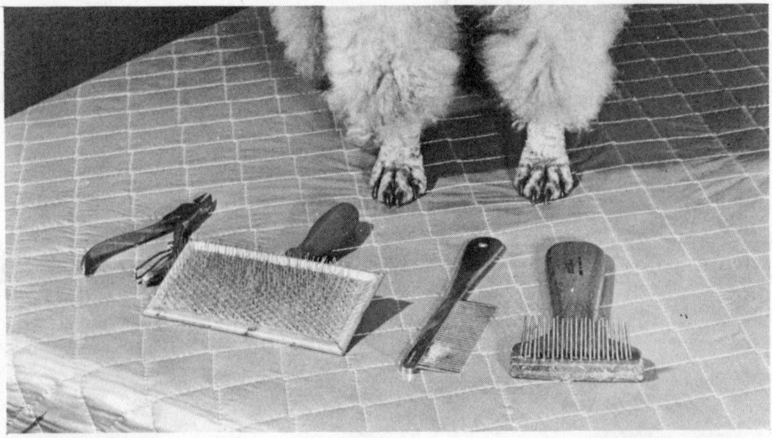

Besides the clipper, a rake, comb, brush and nail clipper are necessary to groom your poodle properly. Let your dog become familiar with these instruments before you use them on him. This prevents the poodle from being frightened by something unknown.

RAKE: Poodles always seem to get tangles and knots which become very matted and require something a little stronger than a comb. A poodle rake is very useful in removing mattings and tangles. Use it humanely. A single or double row of teeth is desirable. More than a double row is too painful for your poodle to tolerate.

NAIL CLIPPER: Special nail clippers are designed for cutting your poodle's nails. Be careful of the vein in your dog's nails when clipping.

BRUSH: A stiff, long-bristled brush is necessary to groom your poodle properly after he has been clipped.

TWEEZERS: In order to remove the hairs from the outer ear of your poodle, you will need the help of a pair of tweezers.

GROOMING TABLE: Unless you can afford a regular grooming table, use any old, sturdy table and cover the top with a rubber mat.

BATHING YOUR POODLE

It is of the utmost importance that you bathe your poodle before you clip him. Bathing not only makes the hair softer and the knots, tangles and mats easier to remove, but it washes away the odor and provides more comfort for the groomer.

There are two ways to bathe your dog. The old way is the washtub method, familiar to all. Fill a tub up to the point where the water reaches the dog's belly when he is standing in it. The temperature should be as warm as if you were bathing a baby. Then use a regular dog soap or dog shampoo and be careful not to get it in his ears, eyes, nose or mouth.

After he has been thoroughly washed, rinse him off with clean water and dry him with a large rough towel. If you have a hair-dryer, use that when

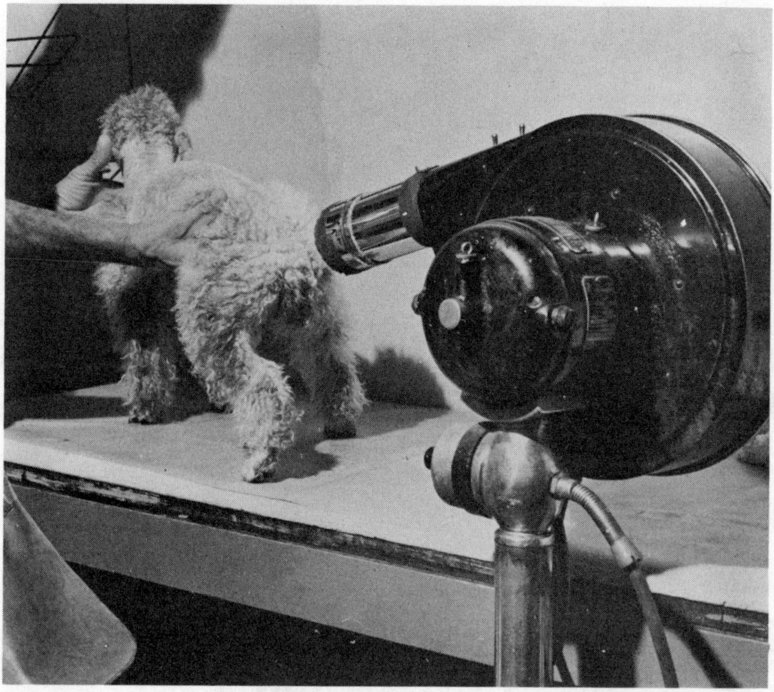

If you have any type of commercial hair dryer use it to dry the coat of your poodle after a bath. Because of the heavy coat for which the poodle is famed, it is essential that you dry it down to the skin.

the weather is cool, though during the summer you might just as well let him dry out in the sun after you've rubbed him down with a heavy towel.

The modern way to bathe your dog is with one of the new "dry cleaners." Some are liquid and some are the foam-type in a pressurized tin can. Merely put the foam onto the dog and rub it in. Then wipe it off with a towel and your dog is clean-looking and clean-smelling. These modern dry cleaners are wonderful, especially in the winter when it is dangerous to bathe your poodle for fear he might catch cold.

Regardless of how you bathe your poodle, remember he must be bathed prior to actual clipping. If you do your own clipping, you will understand why.

THE PUPPY CLIP

The face can be clipped clean or with a moustache. Keep your poodle in a sitting position when clipping his face and use the #10 or #15 blade working against the grain of the hair. Cut an inverted Λ between the eyes of the poodle, going about one inch above an imaginary line drawn between the eyes.

Teach your children to run their fingers through your poodle's coat to search for knots and tangles. This "diagnosis" can be part of your caressing and petting.

Daily brushing, especially if the poodle's hair is long, is the only way to prevent and correct knots and tangles. A special brush is available at your local petshop to assist you.

Clean the throat area and clip towards each ear. Take off all the hair on the throat and under the muzzle. Clip a V shaped area under the throat so when you look into the puppy's face he seems to be wearing an open collar shirt.

Now move to the feet and clip all the hair off the feet to about an inch or so above the ankle bone. Use the edge or corner of the clipper to get in between the toes. (If you use the scissors for this job be very careful.) In clipping the front paws have the poodle in a sitting position; in clipping the back paws, have the dog facing away from you.

Cut the hair on the bottom of the feet too.

The poodle's tail is very important to his appearance. Clip the hair from the base of the tail to about an inch from the end of the tail. After the tail has been cleaned, use a scissors to form the pompom into as round a ball as you can get. Let the pompom grow as long as possible so the dog seems to have a longer tail.

Now brush the poodle thoroughly, fluffing the hair and making it stand out evenly all about his body. If the hair falls into his face you can use a barette or ribbon to fasten the forelocks back.

The puppy clip with moustache.

THE ENGLISH SADDLE CLIP

Clip the face the same way as for the Puppy Clip.

For the front paws begin clipping about 3 inches above the clipped part of the ankle, leaving 3 inches of hair between these trims. Cut the hair until it reaches the joint where the legs meet the poodle's body. Clean off all the hair. The little hair that is left is called a "bracelet." Cut and trim the remaining bracelet to form a round or oval ball. For the rear paws cut a fine band of hair off just above the hock joint. This band should be no smaller than one inch thick and not more than 1½ inches. Trim the hair shorter the closer it gets to the ankle.

Now work on the body of the poodle and, using a #5 blade, remove all but one inch of hair on the back and 2 inches on the sides. Cut the hair until you reach the last rib of the dog, then stop. Now use a #15 blade and cut a band one inch in width all about the body to separate the long hair from the short. Now form the back hair to fit the poodle's body.

Comb and brush and use scissors to get in the final touches.

A toy poodle with a Royal Dutch.

A toy poodle with a Continental Clip.

The poodle above has an English Saddle Clip. The puppy shown below has a Puppy Clip.

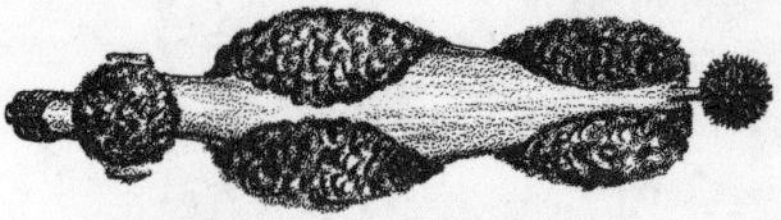

Top view of poodle with Royal Dutch Clip.

The Royal Dutch Clip, though not a show clip, is very popular.

The Continental Clip.

THE CONTINENTAL CLIP

The Continental Clip is a take-off on the English Saddle Clip. Go through the same process as the English Saddle but instead of leaving the hair on the back, remove it as you see in the drawing.

It is interesting to note that the Continental Clip is utilitarian and not just someone's idea of how to make the poodle look pampered. It derives from the days when the poodle was used in hunting and retrieving, and frequently was called upon to swim in icy waters after game. The long coat about his chest protected him in the water while the naked legs gave him more freedom for swimming.

THE ROYAL DUTCH CLIP

The Royal Dutch Clip is frowned upon by so many poodle experts that everybody wants one just to be different! I, personally, think it makes for a beautiful dog and I keep my poodles in the Royal Dutch because it is a simple cut to give and still retains the pampered appearance that poodles have become famous for.

Starting with the Puppy Clip, clean the face, pompom and trimmed feet, follow the shoulder muscles and rear leg muscles and trim the hair inside these boundaries until the dog takes the appearance illustrated here. Then all that's left to be done is the neck, still following the shoulder muscle outline.

You can clip the face higher or lower, like the Puppy Clip or any way that suits your own taste. There are no hard and fast rules to follow with this clip.

The Kennel Clip is a utility clip.

THE KENNEL CLIP

The Kennel Clip is the easiest clip of all and the least that a poodle should get. The idea of this clip is that it is easy to maintain and it allows for any other clip once someone has purchased the dog.

The Kennel Clip is little more than a clipped face. Follow the instructions under the Puppy Clip, leave a pompom on the tail with the hair removed from the rest of the tail.

Poodles kept in the Kennel Clip should be brushed as often as possible and their hair should be kept short by frequent clippings with a #5 blade. The hair on a Kennel-clipped poodle should never be more than 2 inches in length.

The best advice for the novice is to give your poodle to a dog shop that specializes in poodle grooming.

DO'S AND DON'T'S OF CLIPPING YOUR POODLE

Do give your poodle regular grooming so that knots, mats and tangles do not require cutting, thus ruining your poodle's coat for some time to come.

Do try to get assistance the first few times you groom your dog.

Do get proper tools.

Do your clipping in the morning, if possible, when there is plenty of natural light available.

Do groom your dog out of doors on very warm days.

Do hold your poodle's face firmly when working on any part of his head or face.

Do take off a little hair at a time, going over the same area again and again when necessary.

Do follow the instructions carefully.

Do bathe the poodle before you clip him.

Don't use the scissors without being extremely careful.

Don't let any cut go untreated.

Don't stretch the skin on the dog's body (it is permissible to stretch the lips only).

Don't use dull blades.

Don't clip against the grain on the poodle's ears or on his penis.

Don't jam the clippers if they tangle in his coat.

Don't be cruel under any circumstances.

A well-groomed poodle in the Royal Dutch Clip in his own bed. There is a lot to be said for the poodle to have its own bed. It's the place for it to sleep, of course, but it is also its own private place . . . a place where it can retreat if it is not feeling well or has been scolded.

The well groomed poodle has an advantage over almost every other breed of dog. Their coat is so constructed that they almost never lose a hair anyplace in the house. The outer coat holds the loose hair until the poodle is brushed, thus they make exceptional house pets. Samson has just caught his squeak toy in mid-air.

(Above) When using the comb on a tangled poodle coat, don't just dig in and pull as hard as you can. It is just as painful to the dog when you pull his hair as it is pulling your own. (Below) Author Miller humanely holds the ear firmly and works out the tangles gently with a brush.

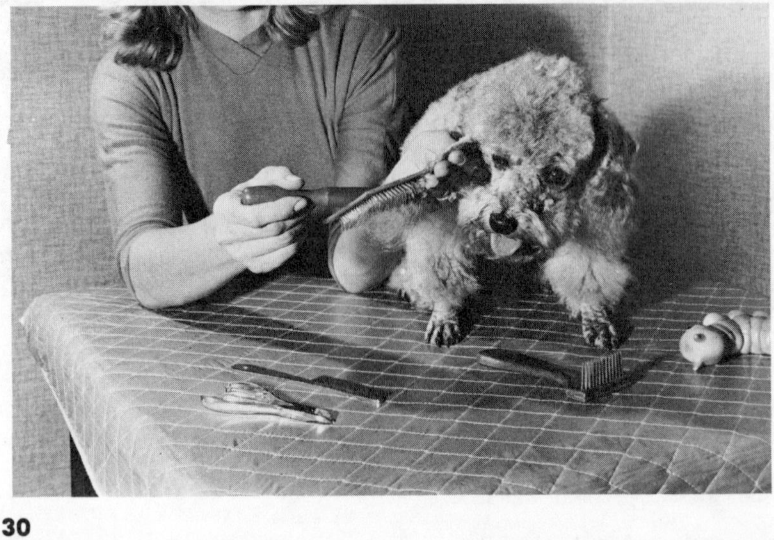

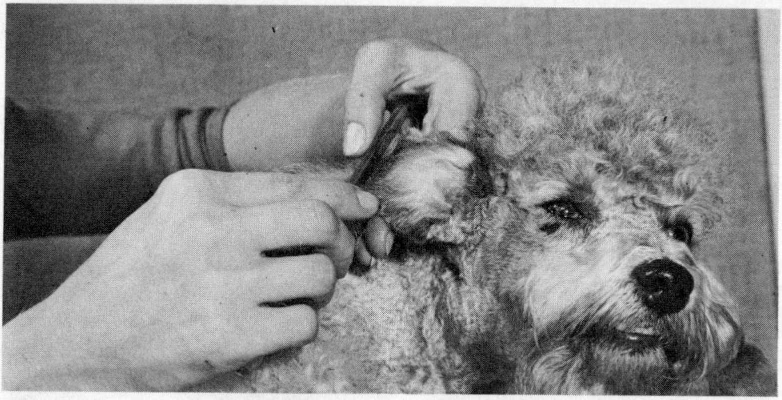

Use great care when combing the underside of the ear. This is probably the most sensitive part of a poodle's body. When the ear is pulled back examine it for a possible discharge that is symptomatic of canker.

4. How to Train Your Dog

ANIMAL OR PET?

There is only a one-word difference between an *animal* and a *pet* and that word is TRAINING.

But training your dog depends upon many factors:

how intelligent you are;
how intelligent the dog is;
what your intentions are;
how much time you are willing to devote to the task.

First we consider the dog owner who is merely interested in training his dog to be a perfect home companion, a dog that he can be proud to own, a dog that won't embarrass him by untimely "accidents" nor kill himself by running into the street.

THE DOG OWNER'S PART

Before you begin training your dog to be a pet, there are certain important facts to remember:

You are a human being and do not speak the same language that a dog does. So you must try to think as a pet dog thinks; your dog will try to understand his trainer.

Training your dog is like training a child. It requires firmness tempered with kindness, strictness but gentleness, consistency, repetition and above all PATIENCE. You must have the patience to go over the training cycle time and time again until the message reaches your dog.

Did you know that a dog is the only known animal that can be bribed into learning by just a few kind words and soft pats on the back? Other animals must be bribed with food or be beaten into submission, but not your pet dog. He wants kindness and attention. Reward him with a pat on the back when he is doing well and you will soon have a dog eager to learn.

Training your poodle NOT to do things is more important than training him to DO things! Samson was trained to fetch his squeak toy . . . but not to go into the goldfish pool where he might drown.

(Right page) This is a portrait of Gigi, the famous silver miniature poodle bred by Norman and June Elliott of Southampton, England, and owned by the author, Evelyn Miller. Gigi always wears a Royal Dutch clip.

(Above) During training, Miss Miller takes Gigi into a wide open field where there is a minimum of distraction. (Below) Gigi, a very alert poodle, has been commanded to STAY where she is. Even though she may be called by name by a stranger, she will not budge from the spot. This is only one of the advantages of having a trained dog. The poodle is the easiest dog to train as it is probably the most intelligent.

When training your poodle use hand signals as well as verbal commands. It is a simple matter to train your dog to understand both if you utilize them during the training period.

GIVING COMMANDS

When you give commands use the shortest phrase possible and use the same word with the same meaning at all times. If you want to teach your dog to sit, then always use the word SIT. If you want your dog to lie down, then always use the word DOWN. It doesn't matter what word you use as long as your dog becomes accustomed to hearing it and acts upon it.

The trick hound dog that always sits on the command UP and stands on the command SIT was easily trained to understand the words that way. The words are merely sounds to him. He cannot understand you but he understands the tone of your voice and the inflection of the words.

Unless you are consistent in your use of commands you can never train your animal properly.

WHAT ABOUT LESSONS?

Try to make your training lessons interesting and appealing both to yourself and your dog. Short frequent lessons are of much more value than long lessons. It is much better for all concerned if you teach your dog for 10 minutes at a time, three times a day, than for 30 minutes once a day. The 10 minute session amuses both you and your dog and the attachment which develops between you during these lessons will be everlasting.

A good time to train your dog is for 10 minutes before you give him his breakfast; then he assumes that the meal is a reward for his being such a good dog. If you follow this schedule for all three meals your training program will be extremely successful.

WHAT YOU WILL TEACH YOUR DOG

Your house pet should certainly learn the rudiments necessary to good behavior. Your dog should be housebroken first of all. Then he should learn how to walk properly with a collar and leash, after which he should be taught the simple commands of HEEL, SIT, COME and STAY. Only after the dog has learned these commands is it safe to train him off the leash.

Once your dog gets into the swing of his training it is wise to continue to train him in more difficult performances. After all, the hardest part of the

This is a baby silver toy poodle. The outer coat is always pitch black at birth. As the puppy gets older the hair gets more silver all the time.

Miss Miller with Gigi. Note Gigi's black nose and brown eyes. The two puppies are a silver and a black. The black puppy is just one ball of fur and that's about all you can see.

job is establishing a communication system so that each of you learns what to expect from the other. Once your dog learns a trick or a command he will hardly ever forget it if you repeat it every so often. Begging, giving his paw, playing dead and rolling over are entertaining tricks which you, your friends and your dog can all enjoy to mutual benefit. There are, however, more important lessons first.

HOW TO HOUSEBREAK YOUR PUPPY

Teaching your dog to relieve himself outdoors or on paper indoors (housebreaking) is the most essential part of his early training. You must begin housebreaking while he is a puppy. Keep in mind the fact that a puppy

If you want to restrain your poodle in one room, use a small gate, like this arrangement found in Miss Miller's home. Your poodle, being a very inquisitive dog, can see what's going on if he becomes interested.

must be fed more often than an adult dog, and consequently must relieve himself more frequently. Housebreaking is not only important from your viewpoint (keeping the house clean) but also from the dog's viewpoint, as no dog can have self-respect and the ability to be trained in other ways if he dirties his own quarters.

Dogs are a lot like some people – they will try to get away with as much as they possibly can. If you let your dog dirty your floor, then he will. If you let him know that you won't put up with this nonsense, then he will obey you. Here are some rules in housebreaking:

Take your dog outside as frequently as possible. If you don't have the time to spend with him outdoors, then obtain a tie-out picket pin from your local store and tie your dog outside until he has performed his duties. Start out as soon after meals as possible because your puppy usually will relieve himself right after he eats. Keep him outdoors until he does his duty. Once he gets used to the idea that he will be allowed indoors again as soon as his duty is completed, he will take care of the job that much sooner. That's about all there is to housebreaking your dog outdoors.

Now let's consider the situation if the weather is very bad or if you live in an apartment house and can't run down all the time to teach your puppy. It is the accepted practice to train a dog to relieve himself on paper in case of emergencies. There are also times when you are going away for the day and won't be around to take your dog out. That's where the paper comes in, too. You certainly don't want him to get sick by not moving his waste, and the poor dog won't know what to do if he's not trained to paper.

Start teaching him about paper, when your puppy is very young and can hardly walk by himself. Take your puppy to the paper every time you catch him in the act. It often helps to blot some of his liquid errors on the paper and leave that soiled paper on top of clean paper so he will get to know that this is the place for him to do his duty. It usually takes about a week.

COLLAR AND LEASH

As soon as you purchase your dog be sure that you stop at your pet shop and pick out the type of collar and leash that best suits your purposes. Leashes are available in many different colors and materials. You can buy a chain leash, a light plastic leash for small breed dogs, or a genuine leather leash for longer, more beautiful wear.

When buying your leash and collar be prepared to order the size you need. If you don't have a tape measure to gauge the collar size of your dog, merely take a piece of string and tie it loosely around your dog's neck. Mark off the distance and take this in with you so your salesman can give you the proper size.

When housebreaking your poodle puppy, take him right from his bed and place him on the previously soiled newspaper. Give him a loving pat when he does his duty properly.

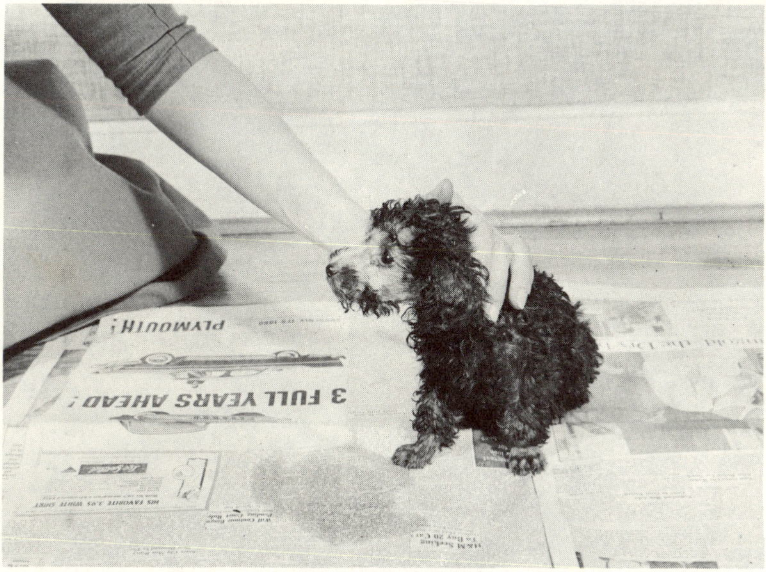

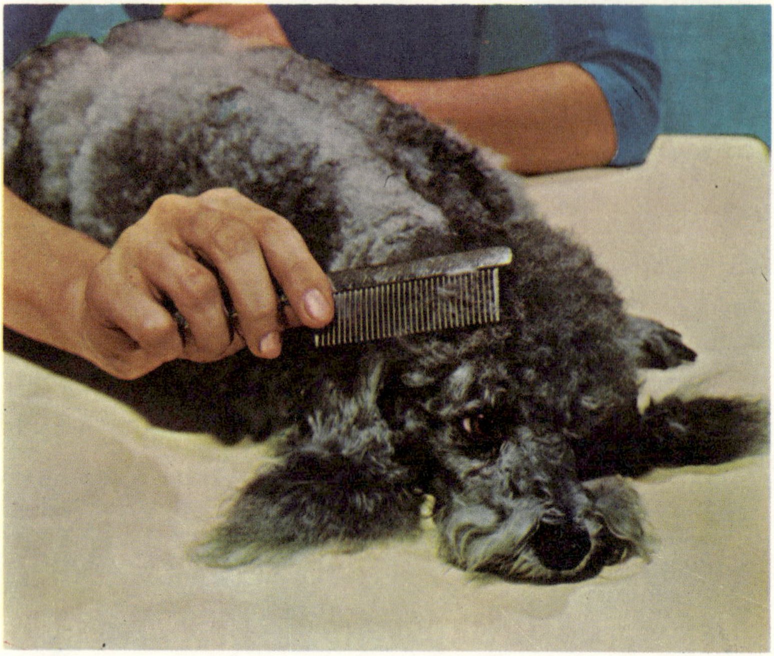

(Above) Gigi poses proudly with her new raincoat. Poodles seem to sense their own pride when adorned with fancy garments, while other breeds might try vigorously to shake off the restraining garb.

(Top, left page) Gigi is spruced up with a brush to make the pompom on her tail a bit more fluffy.

(Bottom, left page) By combing the hair gently and by not taking too deep a "bite" with the comb, you will teach your poodle to enjoy the grooming sessions.

Teach children their responsibility toward their pet. Don't allow your dog to roam about without a lead.

If you decide on a collar for a puppy, buy one that fits nicely when on the tightest hole so that as your dog grows he can grow into the collar. If your dog is older, get one with a fit that takes the collar to the center hole so that fluctuations in his coat can be compensated for with a hole on either side. Collars and harnesses are made to last a long time, so be certain that you get one that your dog will not grow out of.

Once you have the proper size collar (or harness) for your puppy let him sniff it and play with it for a minute or two to get accustomed to the smell of the material. Then gently hold the pup in your arms and slowly put the collar on him. Chances are that he won't like this strange feeling a bit, but don't give in. Just comfort him and play with him for a while and he'll forget all about it. Keep the collar on the dog at all times thereafter, except of course, when you bathe him.

TRAINING YOUR DOG TO WALK PROPERLY

After your dog has been housebroken and has become accustomed to his collar or harness you must teach him to walk properly on a leash. We are assuming that you will use the collar and leash when housebreaking your puppy. Once he is thoroughly familiar with the workings of these restraining objects, you must teach him to respect the master at the other end of the leash.

You should hold the leash firmly in your right hand. The dog should walk on your left side with the leash crossing the front of your body. The reason for this will be obvious once you've actually walked your dog . . . you have more control this way.

Let your dog lead you for the first few moments so that he fully understands that freedom can be his if he goes about it properly. He knows already that when he wants to go outdoors the leash and collar are necessary, so he has respect for the leash. Now, if while walking, he starts to pull in one direction all you do is *stop walking*. He will walk a few steps and then find that he can't walk any further. He will then turn and look into your face. *This is the crucial point*. Just stand there for a moment and stare right back at him . . . Now walk another ten feet and stop again. Again your dog will probably walk out the leash, find he can't go any further, and turn around and look again. If he starts to pull and jerk then just stand there. After he quiets down, just bend down and comfort him as he may be frightened. Keep up this training until he learns not to outwalk you.

You must understand that most dogs like to stop and sniff around a bit until they find THE place to do their duty. Be kind enough to stop and wait when they find it necessary to pause. This is the whole story . . . it's as easy as

Your pet, off leash, might start chasing a cat or running after another dog. Most poodles can easily outrun the fastest human being and they can get lost very easily.

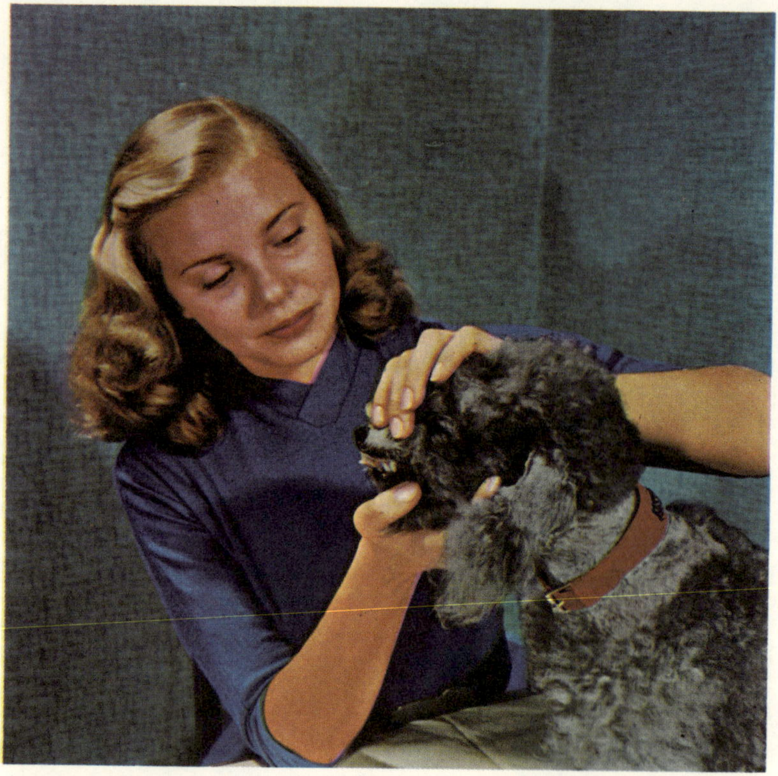

Examine your poodle's teeth regularly. If your dog is properly trained it will be a simple matter to make routine checkups. If your dog is untrained, you might need two people just to hold him while the third person examines.

that. A smart dog can learn to walk properly in a few days, provided you have taught him correctly from the beginning. A dog that is incorrectly trained initially may take a month to retrain, but in any event, every dog can learn to walk properly on a leash!

TRAINING YOUR DOG TO COME TO YOU

Your dog has been named and he knows his name. After hearing his name called over and over again in your home, he finds that it pays to come when called. Why? Because you only call him when his food is ready or when you wish to play with him and pet him. Outside the house it is a different story. He would rather play by himself or with other dogs or chase a cat than play with you. So, he must be trained to come to you when he is called. Here's how to do it:

After you have trained your pet to walk properly on a leash let him walk out the entire length of the leash. Then stop and call him to you. If he just stands there looking up with those soulful eyes that made you buy him in the first place, then gently pull on the leash until he comes to your feet, even if you have to drag him over. By no means should you walk to him! If you have some "candy" for dogs, which you can get at your pet shop, give him one after you've pulled him to you. Pat his head, making a big fuss over him as though you haven't seen him for weeks!

Then walk along and try it all over again. Repeat the process until he finally gets the idea. It shouldn't take long if you are consistent about it every time you take him out for his walk. Don't forget the dog candy because if you get him to learn that a satisfactory performance earns him a piece, the more difficult lessons will be easier to get across.

TRAINING YOUR DOG TO STAY AT YOUR SIDE

From here on, the training gets a bit more difficult. So far the house-breaking, walking and coming when called has constituted the basic training EVERY dog must know. What follows is more difficult to teach and is harder for the dog to learn because it means he has to give up some of his freedom and playfulness.

To train your dog to stay by your side is a little harder than to train

A silver poodle (right) and a black. These puppies would look identical if they didn't have their faces trimmed. All silver puppies should be trimmed at an early age to promote the growth of their silver coat.

If your poodle misbehaves during training, give him a severe tongue lashing. Poodles as a rule have easy-going temperaments and usually take a scolding to heart. Believe it or not, you can easily hurt their feelings by unwarranted scoldings.

him not to pull on the leash. For the "heel training" you must get another type collar – *a choke chain collar*. It is made of polished, chrome chain and it is designed to tighten about your dog's neck if he pulls too hard. The collar is definitely not a cruel instrument (as the name might imply). Here's what you do:

Put the choke chain collar on your dog the next time you take him out. If he pulls too hard, this type collar will definitely break that habit one, two, three! Once you've gotten him accustomed to the action of the choke chain collar stop the walk and start out again with the dog's nose even with your left knee. Walk quickly, repeating as you go the word HEEL over and over again. If your dog walks out past your knee, jerk him back firmly, but not *cruelly,* raising your voice HEEL at the same time. If he persists in going out in front of you all the time, stop and start all over again. Repeat this process until he learns it . . . Have patience, for once he learns to walk by your side in this manner, you will have a well-mannered dog all his life.

Some dogs are a bit lazy and will walk behind you instead of in front of you. If your dog does this, stop and call him to you and keep calling him with the word HEEL until he finally gets the idea. After each proper performance offer him some dog candy. Keep your dog informed that the word HEEL means he is to walk close to your left heel.

After your dog has learned to HEEL on a tight lead, you can use a slack

In training your dog to sit, first place him in the sitting position and then keep your hand raised while repeating the command SIT.

leash and let him wear his normal, everyday collar. If he forgets himself, put the choke chain collar on again right away. Don't give him a chance to forget his lessons . . . and don't forget to use the same word HEEL at all times.

TRAINING YOUR DOG TO STOP WITHOUT COMMAND

When your dog has been trained to HEEL on a loose leash, the next step in his training is to STOP without command so that if you stop for a street corner or to talk to someone along the way, your dog doesn't pull you to get going. Training to stop without command requires use of the choke chain collar for the first lessons.

Take your dog out for his usual walk, keeping him at HEEL all the time. Then stop dead in your tracks keeping the leash tight in your hands without a bit of slack. DO NOT LET HIM SIT DOWN! No command is necessary. As soon as he stops, pat him on the back and give him some dog candy. Then walk on again briskly and stop short. Keep your dog on the tight leash at all times and repeat this until he learns that he must stop dead in his tracks just as you do. When you stop, stop *deliberately* so that he can actually anticipate your stopping and be with you at all times. You can tell when he is being attentive for he will walk a few steps and then turn his head so that he can keep an eye on your face. He will actually crave to satisfy you once he has

Teaching your dog to BEG is simple. Start from the sitting position and hold a piece of dog candy slightly above his head. Begging will come naturally. All poodles are born actors!

been properly taught, and he will only take a few steps before he swings his head to look at you. Next time you see a well-trained dog walking along the street, notice how much time he spends looking at his master instead of at other things.

Once your dog has learned to stop without command and you want to walk again, you can signal him by many means. One way is to slacken your leash and then start walking so that he will learn that a slackened leash means you intend to walk again. Another way is to signal him verbally with the word "Go" or "Come on Pal" or something similar to that. It doesn't matter what word you use as long as you use the same word all the time.

OFF-THE-LEASH TRAINING

After your dog has accomplished these lessons it is time to begin his training without a leash. Try to find a large open area which is fenced in. It will be safer to advance to this stage within the confines of that area. If no such area is available, find as quiet a street as you can (even late at night so that few automobiles are around) and begin your training there.

Let's assume that your dog heels and stops without command. After you've walked him a few feet and tested him on stopping without command, bend down and remove the leash. Start walking briskly as you did when training him to heel. Stop suddenly without command and see if he does the same. If he doesn't, then immediately snap on the leash with the choke collar and go through the training again. Walk once with the leash on and once with the leash off, until finally your dog gets the idea that he can have more freedom by behaving himself, than misbehaving. Don't forget to carry some dog candy along with you so you can reward him for a successful performance.

It is important for you and your dog to use his regular collar during "off-training" hours, since your dog likes a recess every few days. Then when you put on the training collar he knows that something new is coming along. Every time you put on the training collar give him a piece of candy and an extra pat or two. Let him know that both of you are going to enjoy the new experience.

TEACHING YOUR DOG TO SIT

Once your dog has mastered the art of heeling with a regular collar, put on his choke chain collar and start a new lesson.

After a brisk walk go through the previous lessons as far as the short stop, your dog will be standing watching you and waiting for the loose leash to walk on further. When you reach this point, gently push his hind quarters down with your left hand as you hold the leash tightly raised in your right hand. This will keep his head up and his butt down. Don't let him lie all the way down or cower. Use just enough pressure so he knows to sit. Once he's in the sitting position give him a piece of dog candy, a few pats on the head and start walking again.

Do this several times. He should go into the sitting position every time you want him to, provided you let him know when you want him to sit.

Remember that when you stopped your dog was standing at your side ready to go off again whenever you were ready. Now use the word SIT very often so he can accustom his ears to *that* sound. Every time you push his hindquarters down, say SIT. Keep repeating this word over and over again as you push him down. Soon he will learn when he should sit and when he should stay close to your side when you stop for a short time.

After thoroughly training your dog in sitting with a leash, go through the same method of training without a leash. A simple method is to walk along briskly, stop and tell him to SIT. As soon as he sits take the leash off and walk again. Then stop and tell him to SIT again.

If he doesn't sit upon command, hold his choke chain in your hand and force his hindquarters down into the sitting position. Do this again and again until he learns. As soon as he gets it right, give him a piece of dog candy. Repeat this training until it is thoroughly ingrained in his habits. It is always important to keep in mind that you must never start a new lesson until the old one is mastered. Inconsistency on your part is considered a weakness by your dog.

TRAINING YOUR DOG TO LIE DOWN

Now that your dog can sit with a leash or without a leash and is thoroughly familiar with your training routine, perhaps you want to train him to lie down. Many people feel that there is no reason for teaching him to lie down and they don't bother, but if you want him to ride safely in an automobile, training in lying down is important.

Usually DOWN is the command word for lying down although any word you use will be acceptable, provided you use the same word to have the same meaning every time you use it.

Take your dog out and go through the training sequence until you have him in a sitting position. Then walk in front of him and gently pull his two front paws forward so that he automatically falls into the lying down position. As you do this say DOWN. If he raises his hindquarters then use the command SIT and his hindquarters should drop immediately. Only constant repetition of this exercise will finally get him to lie down immediately upon command.

It is very helpful to use a hand signal along with the verbal command

Everyone likes to "show off" their trained poodles. Imagine how thrilling it is to have a trained dog that can really put on an act when prompted! The increased value of a trained dog over an untrained animal is fantastic.

DOWN. The usual hand signal is to extend your left hand, with your palm down, as a sign to lie down. A very successful variation is merely to point down as you give the order. Any signal is satisfactory as long as you are consistent.

When giving the hand signal be careful that your dog doesn't think you are threatening him. You can dispel this fear by immediately offering him some dog candy each time he successfully completes the lying down maneuver.

TEACHING YOUR DOG TO STAY

The main objective in teaching your dog to sit and lie down is to get him to stay where you want him. Many times you will restrict him to a certain room, possibly the kitchen. When the front door rings, you don't want him tracking through the house. Will you have to lock him in the kitchen before you open the front door? Do you want him to follow you all over the house whenever you move from room to room? If the answer to these questions is to be "No!," then he must be trained to stay.

Then again, what more beautiful sight is there than to see a dog "parked" outside a supermarket (while his master is buying dog candy!) waiting in a sitting or lying down position. No one but his master's command can budge him. Though strangers may pat him and entice him, nothing can make him move from the position he is in. These are some of the rewards you receive by training.

To train your dog to stay is not a difficult feat at all. Once he sits or lies upon command, proceed with the STAY command. Immediately after he is seated (or lying down) drop the leash and walk away three or four steps. Keep facing him while you are doing this, and, if he starts to rise to follow you, raise your voice and give the hand signal DOWN! If he doesn't get down immediately, walk back to him very briskly and force him down in no uncertain manner. Then try again to walk a few feet from him. Repeat this sequence until he finally stays at the command. The following day walk a little bit further; keep up this training until finally you can walk away, out of sight, and he will stay where he is, waiting for you.

When you want your dog to rise out of the position he is in, command COME (or call his name, whichever way you have decided earlier in his training). Do not allow him to run to you from the STAY position because you return to his line of vision. He must await your permission to come to you. This part of the training either makes or breaks a dog. The test is simple for an obedient, well disciplined dog. If you are lax and inconsistent in the initial stages, then it will be impossible to train him to stay.

DISCIPLINE TRAINING FOR YOUR DOG

Up to this point you have been training your dog to act upon command. Now you will attempt to train his intelligence. This is another important part of the training problem and it is the part that separates a "smart" dog from one that doesn't "use his head."

All dogs, regardless of their training, will get the urge to run after

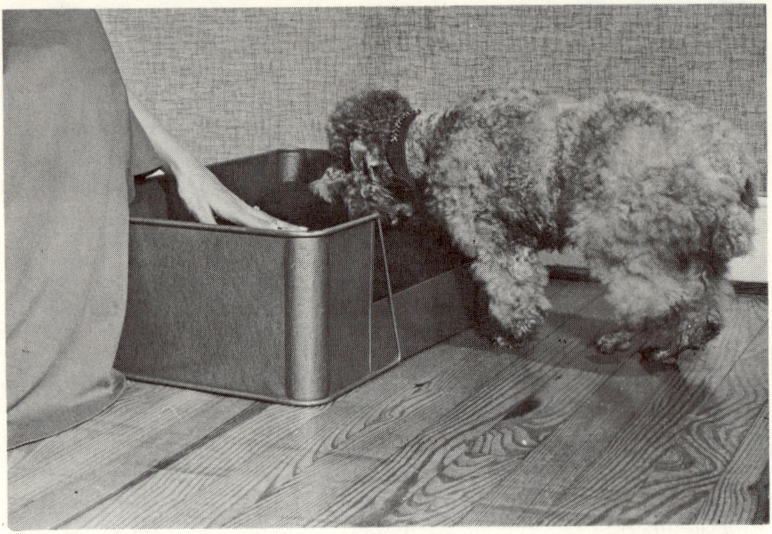

If your poodle misbehaves while in the house, a severe tongue lashing should send her scampering back to bed. Train her to go to her bed when she misbehaves. This is Gigi and she isn't wasting any time!

another dog, to chase a cat, to fetch, or just to run for the sheer love of running. In the open field or park this is perfectly all right, but in the city it can be catastrophic! Let's assume that your dog has a bad habit of slipping off his collar and making a mad dash away from you. You may find this out some fine, bright morning when both of you are in fine spirits: He will spot a cat, and without warning will dash off, either pulling the leash right out of your unwary hands or slipping his head out of the collar. A moment of panic will hit you both. But, once the initial impact of the moment is over, he will come scampering back at the command COME.

At this point do not beat your dog. He knows he has done something wrong and he is a bit confused himself. Just pat him on the head and ignore it . . . *this time.* Then walk back to the house and get a long rope, 25 to 30 feet long. Tie this rope to his regular collar (do not use a choke chain) and also use the regular leash. Try to get your dog into the same situation as the one he bolted from. When he runs away from you again (if he does), drop the leash but hold onto the rope. When he gets far enough away give a loud holler STOP and jerk the rope at the same time. He will spin in his tracks and lay where he is, thoroughly confused and a bit scared.

Go over to him and make a big fuss over him as though you can't imagine what happened. Tell him he should never have left your side. Repeat this training four or five times and he will never bolt from you again.

You can practice the command STOP by running a few steps with him and then shouting the command STOP as you suddenly stop short. By repeating the command STOP in every such situation it won't be too long before you can make your dog STOP on a dime!

KEEPING YOUR DOG OFF THE FURNITURE

Your favorite sofa or chair will also be your dog's favorite seat. It is naturally used the most and so will have the odors (which only your dog can smell) of the beloved master. There are two ways of training your dog out of the habit of sitting in your chair. (You will want to break the habit because most dogs shed and their hair gets all over your clothes. Then again, he might like to curl up in your lap while you are trying to read or knit.)

The simplest way of breaking the habit is to soak a small rag with a special dog scent which is repulsive to dogs. Put the rag on the chair which your dog favors. He will jump on the chair, get a whiff of the scent and make a detour of the chair forever more!

Another way to train is to pull him off the chair every time you catch him there and immediately command him to lie DOWN at your feet. Then give him a severe tongue lashing. After a few times he will never go to the chair again WHILE YOU ARE AROUND! The greater problem is to teach

Miss Miller is quite peeved that Gigi has made herself comfortable in a favorite chair. Since poodles are one of the few dogs that do not shed at any time of the year if properly groomed, it is no great catastrophe if she jumps onto the furniture from time to time.

him to stay away all the time. The usual plan is to get a few inexpensive mouse traps and set them (without bait of course) with a few sheets of newspaper over them. As soon as your dog jumps onto the chair the mouse-trap goes SNAP and off the chair goes the dog. He may try it again, but then the second trap will go off, and he will have learned his lesson.

Since your dog has his own bed, train him to stay in it when you don't want him to be any place else. This can be done by saying the word BED in a loud voice and dragging him over and placing him in it. Do this a few times and he will learn where to go when you want him in bed!

TRAINING YOUR DOG NOT TO BARK

For people who live close to another family, a barking dog is a nuisance and your dog must be trained not to bark unless he hears a very strange sound or sees a stranger on your premises. Do not forget that barking is to a dog what a voice is to a human and he expresses happiness, alarm, pain and warning in his bark. It would be impossible to write down all the different sounds that a dog can make, but you will recognize the difference between a whimper, a growl, a howl and a bark. A whimper denotes pain or discomfort. A growl denotes danger and is a warning. A howl denotes loneliness and a bark denotes strange sounds.

To break your dog of excess barking merely requires the use of a rolled newspaper. Every time he barks for some unknown reason, or barks excessively when strangers approach, swat your own hand smartly with the rolled paper, making as loud a smack as possible and at the same time command QUIET. This has never failed to stop a dog. You must repeat this every time he howls.

Certain dogs, regardless of training or breeding, howl and bark all night long and nothing short of chloroform can stop them. If you muzzle him, it may fail to stop the howling, too. There are then only two choices open to the dog owner. Either he gives the dog to a farmer who doesn't mind the howling all night, until finally the howler grows up; or a veterinarian can "debark" the dog by removing the dog's vocal chords. Though veterinarians say this is not a cruel thing to do, it is up to the individual to make his own decision.

TRAINING YOUR DOG TO DO TRICKS

Nearly every housedog learns a few tricks without training during the course of his puppyhood. These are usually accidentally learned, but the master observes the dog doing them and then prompts him to repeat the same thing over and over again.

You will deliberately want to train your dog to shake hands. First get him into the sitting position. Then upon the command PAW, lift his paw in your hand and shake it vigorously without knocking him off balance. Then give him a piece of dog candy. Repeat this several times a day and in a week he will all but hold out his paw when you walk in the door!

Teaching your dog to beg is done in the same manner. Place him in the

Once you have trained your dog to the essentials, you can try some trick-training. Here Gigi is playing hard-to-get. On signal she ignores every command from her trainer regardless of the enticement offered her.

sitting position with the proper command. Then lift his front paws up until he is in a begging position. Hold him that way until he finds a comfortable balance and then let him balance himself. As he gets his balance, hold a piece of dog candy right over his nose. As soon as you let go of his front paws, lower the dog candy to his mouth and let him take it from your hands. Hold the dog candy firmly so it takes a few seconds for him to pry it loose, during this time you are saying BEG, over and over. From then on, you must bribe him with dog candy until he assumes the begging position upon the command BEG. Repeat the preliminary training until he eagerly goes into the begging position to earn dog candy.

TRAINING YOUR DOG TO RETRIEVE

Most dogs are born retrievers and their natural instinct is to chase something that moves. First go to a pet shop and pick out a rubber toy. Try a rubber ball, a rubber bone, anything that attracts your eye. They are all made of completely harmless rubber and are safe even if your dog chews them up.

Then take your dog outside and throw the toy a few feet. He will usually chase it and pick it up. If he doesn't, then you must walk him over to the toy and place it in his mouth and walk him back to your starting position with it. Repeat this operation until he learns the game. Once he goes after the toy, call him to you. If he drops it along the way merely send him back for it by pointing to the object. If necessary, walk him back to the toy, put it in his mouth and walk back with him to the original starting position. When he successfully brings back the object you can reward him with a piece of dog candy.

TRAINING YOUR DOG NOT TO JUMP ON PEOPLE

Some dogs are so affectionate that they will jump on everybody who comes into sight in order to get their attention and affection. Only you can train your dog not to jump and it's an easy trick to learn. As he jumps up to greet *you*, merely bend your knee so he hits it with his chest and falls over. He cannot see your knee coming up as his head will be above your knee. After a few falls he will get the idea that it isn't practical to jump up to greet you or anyone.

Of course if he has learned the meaning of the command DOWN, then use that command when he jumps up. He won't like to assume the down position when he is anxious for a pat or piece of dog candy, so this will be an easy lesson for him to learn.

5. How to Keep Your Poodle Healthy

It's much easier to keep your dog healthy than to have to treat him for any of the ailments that can plague a dog who has been mistreated. Rather than list symptoms and cures let's discuss the various illnesses to which dogs may become victims, and try to understand how to prevent them. While we will discuss treatments, they will be for emergency use – you must always consult your veterinarian as quickly as possible if your dog becomes sick.

A dog needs little care, but that little is essential to his good health and well-being. A dog needs:

1. Proper diet at regular hours
2. Clean, adequate housing
3. Daily exercise
4. Companionship and love
5. Frequent brushing and possibly a bath now and then

If you give your dog these few essentials, chances are that he will never be a sick dog.

EATING FOREIGN PARTICLES

Some dogs have a habit of picking up things in their mouths and tasting them for palatability. If the taste is good the dog will eat the thing, even if it happens to be a spoon with which something delicious was handled. Sooner or later your dog might eat almost anything – pieces of wood, hairpins, shoelaces or rubber balls. This does not usually mean that the dog is starving, but rather that he is bored and doesn't know what to do with himself. If *your* dog shows signs of chewing on everything in sight, give him something special to chew on, like hard dog bones (available from your butcher or from your pet shop), teething toys or an old shoe which you have boiled to rid it of possible harmful dyes or poisons.

Sometimes a dog may eat something which it cannot pass through its digestive tract. This must be removed surgically. If your dog vomits occasionally from eating some of this foreign material, then don't worry too much about it, but if he continually gags or vomits for an extended period of time, get advice from your vet. If your dog eats too much bone, he may become constipated from it and require a dog laxative from time to time.

LOSS OF APPETITE

A dog's appetite is usually directly related to his general health. A dog will refuse to eat for many psychological reasons (new environment, loss of a close friend, a severe scolding, etc.), but most of the time loss of appetite signifies something organically wrong.

A normal, mature dog will eat only one meal a day. If your dog only nibbles on his food, when normally he would gobble it right down, you should look further for symptoms. Sometimes lack of appetite is due to insufficient exercise, or constipation. If your dog *persists* in refusing food you can be certain that something is physically wrong and a professional opinion is needed.

Do you eat when you're not hungry? Well, a dog won't. All breeders and handlers agree that it is best not to feed a dog too much food at each meal. Give him a little bit, always keeping him hungry enough to gobble anything you offer him. Though it's hard to give an exact formula for feeding quantities, you might measure the amount this way: give him only the quantity he will eat without leaving the feeding area.

TOOTH DISORDERS

By the time your dog is a half-year old he will have lost all his baby teeth (he usually eats them) and will have grown most of his permament teeth. Assuming your dog has been fed a well-balanced diet, has had a proper teething bone, and has not been sick, his teeth should make you envious.

If your dog has bleeding gums, impacted teeth or tartar accumulated about the base of his teeth, consult your vet. He can easily correct the situation.

Tartar is a normal phenomenon, but if it is left uncleaned it can easily lead to gum infection. Make a habit of bringing your dog to your vet twice a year for teeth cleaning, nail clipping, ear cleaning and a thorough physical examination.

EAR DISORDERS

Dogs, like humans, have ear tubes that are dead-end streets. In these tubes dust, dirt, wax, hair and mites can accumulate. If you do not clean your dog's ears regularly you can expect trouble. You can clean his ears with some mild soapy cotton. Use the end of a cloth or your finger with the cotton. DO NOT JAB THE COTTON IN WITH A SHARP INSTRUMENT.

If the ear has an odor or you see a pus-like discharge, call your vet. If you notice little mites moving around the ear tube, get your vet in right away. He will be able to prescribe an oil which smothers the mites.

Your dog's ears are as important to him as yours are to you. Take care of them for him.

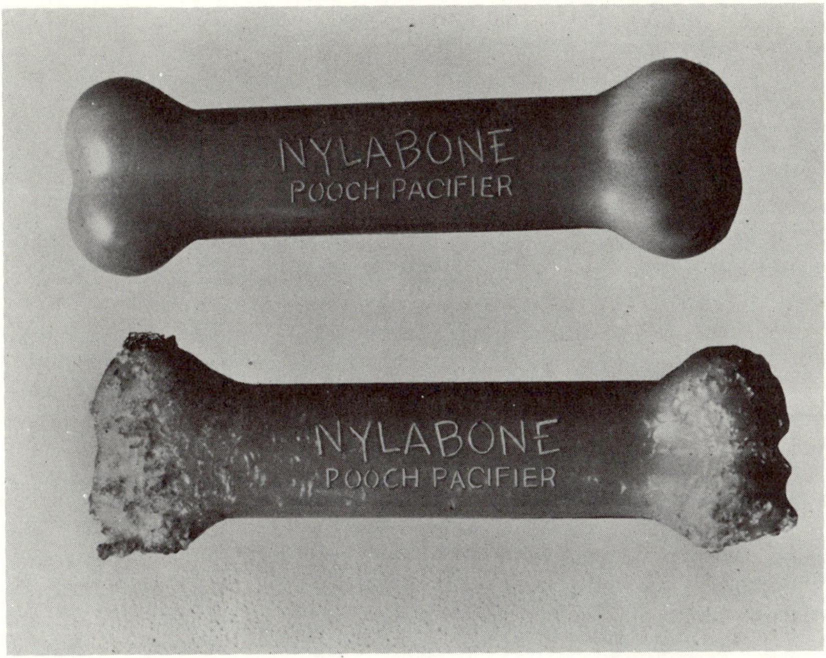

NYLABONE® is a necessity that is available at your local petshop (not in supermarkets). The puppy or grown dog chews the hambone flavored nylon into a frilly dog toothbrush, massaging his gums and cleaning his teeth as he plays. Veterinarians highly recommend this product . . . but beware of cheap imitations which might splinter or break.

MANGE

There are two basic types of mange. Both are caused by parasites that are microorganisms. The first type, and probably the most difficult to cure, is demodectic (follicular) mange. In this ailment the parasite works its way into the skin and surrounding tissue of the hair roots. Intense burning and itching results, causing the dog to bite and scratch himself very severely. Large hairless patches will mark the site of infection. Treatment and cure are very difficult, so consult your vet.

Sarcoptic mange is also called "scabies." It is caused by a small insect that looks like a small crab. This "crab" digs in just under the skin and makes life miserable for the unfortunate dog. Consult your vet for treatment. BOTH TYPES OF MANGE ARE COMMUNICABLE.

VOMITING

Vomiting can be the result of overeating, travel sickness or bad food. It can also be the symptom of his having eaten poison, or some indigestible foreign matter. Most of the time a dog will vomit up something that doesn't agree with him. Once he gets it up, he will be fine. If, however, vomiting persists and blood or bile comes up, you must call in a vet. Sometimes milk of magnesia will be helpful in settling his stomach. Give about a teaspoonful for a small dog and twice as much for a fully-grown, mature dog.

LOOSE BOWELS

Loose bowels, or diarrhea, is a very common ailment with most newly-acquired dogs. The change in diet, the excitement, overfeeding, all have a part in this. Diarrhea distresses not only the dog, but also his master.

The best way to stop diarrhea is with milk of bismuth, kaopectate (an apple derivative), or another similar medication sold at your pet supplier.

Sometimes a dog will have persistent diarrhea. This is a very serious symptom and you must suspect worms or even distemper. If your pet seems to have loose bowels all the time, seek advice from your veterinarian.

CONSTIPATION

A well-balanced diet is necessary for a healthy dog. Food that is too rich or too starchy might cause a binding of the bowels. Unless your dog is properly exercised and given regular opportunity to relieve himself, he may become constipated.

Your pet supplier will have handy dog laxatives to recommend. A mild lubricant (a teaspoonful of mineral oil) will also help the situation. If relief is not forthcoming from these sources, consult your vet.

ANUS SCRAPING

A dog has special anal glands on both sides of his rectum. These glands fill up at times and may itch and burn your dog to distraction. Usually he will try to relieve himself by dragging his rear quarters along the ground. If he can apply sufficient pressure at the correct spot the glands will empty out. If itching persists, have your veterinarian empty the glands. He can do this very easily.

Do not make the mistake that many people do. This reaction to an itchy rectum is not the result of worms! Worm medicine will not alleviate the condition.

LICE, FLEAS AND TICKS

Dogs are sometimes afflicted with external parasites. Depending upon the intensity of the infestation, you might easily cope with the situation yourself.

First treat your dog with a suitable powder for fleas. Buy a special powder for lice and ticks at your local pet shop. The directions for its use are on the package. After a few days using the powder, change your dog's sleeping quarters. Wash the bedding material in disinfectant or throw it away. At the same time, bathe your dog with a strong disinfectant type, parasite-killing dog soap. There is also an excellent liquid that may be placed in the rinse water that will kill fleas, lice and ticks. If this does not rid your dog of parasites then consult your veterinarian.

External parasites are rarely dangerous in themselves, but they cause a dog such great discomfort that his entire personality is liable to change. The best insurance against this is to take immediate action when your dog starts incessant scratching.

INTERNAL PARASITES (WORMS)

Every dog during some stage of his life will become a victim of worm parasites. These worms live inside the dog's body, usually in the intestines where they rob the dog of a great deal of its food.

It is important to know what type of worm is living in your pet as some worms must be treated differently than others. If you are fortunate enough to see the worms (or pieces of them) in the dog's stool or in his vomit, study them so you can report their size and shape to the vet or pet supplier.

A puppy might actually swell up because he is so infested with worms. Adult dogs may swell too, but more likely they will lose weight, become listless and finally, if not treated, die of malnutrition or pneumonia (because of their weakened condition). As soon as you suspect your dog has worms, "worm" him. There is a medication that you can purchase at your pet shop. The size capsule you must use depends upon the weight of the dog, so be sure to know approximately what your dog weighs. Follow carefully the instructions on the label.

ECZEMA

Eczema is a general term applied to loss of hair or rash caused by poor diet, an allergy, an infection or poor grooming. The "dry" eczema starts with a scaly, persistent dandruff which progresses to a balding of the infected area. "Wet" or "moist" eczema is usually the result of an allergy. It itches and burns your dog to such a degree that he will scratch himself until he bleeds. If the area is within biting range he may even tear bits of flesh from the infected area, so intense is the discomfort.

Successful treatment for eczema is predicated upon finding the cause of the malady and preventing your dog from scratching and biting himself, before he causes a serious local infection. It is essential that you consult your veterinarian. Sometimes it is considered more humane to put the dog to sleep. Let your vet advise you.

DISTEMPER

Distemper to a dog is like cancer to a human being, a horrible, often fatal, disease. All types of distemper cause the body temperature of the dog to rise. The eyes discharge a mucous secretion and the nose runs profusely. Sometimes diarrhea, prolonged and bloody, follows an attack.

Distemper is caused by a virus, the smallest living cell we know, much smaller than a bacterium. There are cures for some types of distemper but there is a preventative that is much safer and less costly! If you value your dog's life, immunize him against distemper by a series of injections. Consult your vet as soon as you have purchased your puppy.

The simplest and most easily cured form of distemper is the skin type. It manifests itself by the appearance of an abundance of postules on the body of the dog.

Nervous distemper results in severe fits and convulsions. Paralysis and death usually follow. This form of distemper is usually a secondary infection to one of the other forms of distemper. Most veterinarians will request permission to destroy your dog once paralysis sets in. Even those few dogs that may survive the paralysis are left with chorea, a palsied condition, which makes their muscles so weak that they fall off their feet from time to time.

Respiratory and intestinal distemper are other forms of distemper. The respiratory form affects the nasal and sinus passages as well as the lungs and bronchi. The intestinal form affects the alimentary tract. Though these may not be fatal if they are treated with miracle drugs (streptomycin, penicillin, etc.), they are usually followed by nervous distemper.

RABIES

Rabies is the most fatal disease to which a dog may fall victim. It is incurable when it reaches a certain stage and is highly contagious when a dog or person is bitten by an infected animal. But, it is possible to immunize your dog against rabies. Consult your local veterinarian for advice on the type of injections he recommends. There are two known types of rabies: furious and dumb. The furious rabies manifests itself very dramatically. The dog goes wild, running in all directions and biting anything and everything in its path. A rabid dog has even been known to savagely attack the tires on an automobile, tearing his mouth and losing his teeth in the process. After this fit the infected dog usually convulses and dies.

The dumb rabies affects the infected animal in a very different manner. This type of rabid dog cowers in the corner and appears to be just downhearted and "blue." Finally the dog will die. Sometimes a dog infected with dumb rabies might snap at the person who approaches him.

Rabies is as fatal to man and some other animals as it is to dogs. The only time diagnosis can be obtained with certainty is after the animal has been killed and the brain examined by a trained pathologist. If you suspect your dog or any other animal of having rabies, do not destroy him. He must be kept under observation and studied. Call your doctor, veterinarian or local health authority if you suspect a rabies case.

If you are ever bitten by any dog, report it immediately. Rabies can be cured by a very complicated and uncomfortable procedure, provided the disease has not reached beyond a certain point. Have the dog placed under observation to ascertain whether he is rabid or not. Remember: Rabies is fatal if unchecked. Play it safe and report every dog bite.

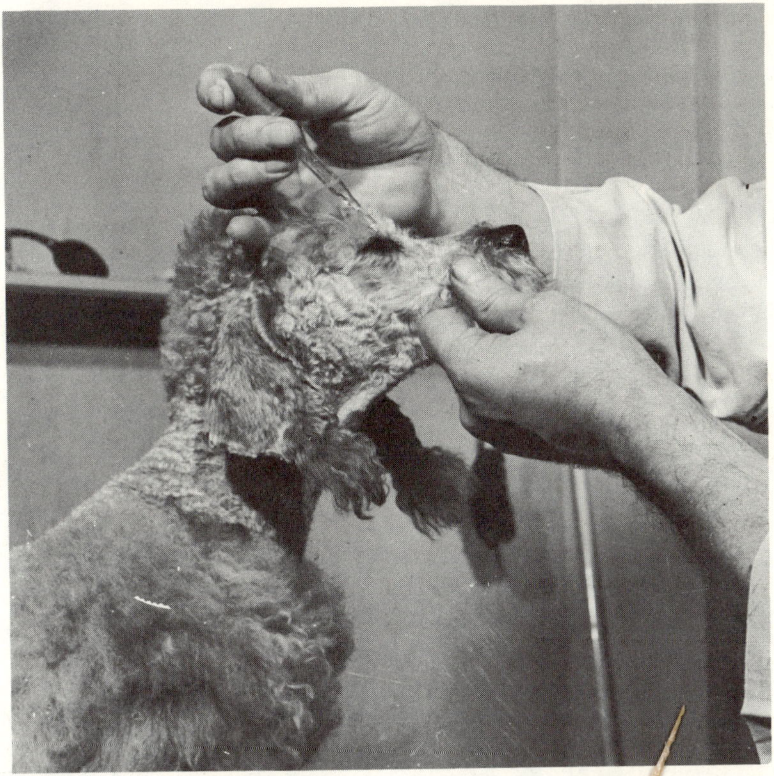

Sometimes a poodle will have running eyes. If this happens to your dog take him to the local veterinarian immediately and have his eyes treated. Running eyes can be the symptom of many serious disorders.

FITS

Dogs occasionally have fits or convulsions which in a few hours disappear and seem to leave the dog none the worse. This type of disorder may be the result of any one of many possible disorders. Dogs have been known to have fits because of rabies, epilepsy, distemper, worms, overheating, indigestion, a foreign object stuck somewhere in the digestive tract, fright or nervousness. Frequent fits over an extended period indicate some basically serious disease. Place the dog in a cool, safe, dark room and call your veterinarian.

HOW TO WEIGH YOUR DOG

The fluctuation in your dog's weight is important as a checkpoint in his health. Worms, external parasites, faulty diet and other disorders manifest themselves by affecting his general health. By checking your dog's weight periodically you can foresee serious consequences of a long unattended ailment.

The easiest method of weighing your dog is to hold him in your arms and step on the scale. After you have noted the combined weight of yourself and your dog, weigh yourself alone. The difference between the two weights is the weight of your dog.

YOUR VETERINARIAN

Your local vet is your best friend. You should consult him when you buy your dog. List his telephone number in your telephone book in case of emergency. Consult him for any major ailment that may affect your dog.

Remember this: *It is better to be safe than sorry!*